Watermarks

Gina Moreno

Alabaster & Mercury Publishing
Ocean Beach, California

Watermarks

Moreno, Gina
Watermarks / Gina Moreno p. cm
ISBN-13: 978-0615921501 (paper : alk. paper)
ISBN-10: 0615921507 (paper : alk. paper)
Copyright © 2010 by Gina Moreno.
Registered In the Library of Congress

Editor: Larry Kuechlin

All rights reserved. Printed in the United States of America. No part of this book may be used or reproduced in any manner whatsoever without the express written permission except in the case of brief quotations embodied in critical articles and reviews.

First Edition. First Pressing, January 2010
Second Edition, November, 2013

Published by:

Alabaster & Mercury Publishing
Ocean Beach, California, USA

5050 Del Monte Ave. #6
San Diego, CA 92107

Printed by BK Printers
Ocean Beach, California

Front cover photo by Larry Kuechlin
Back cover photo by Belliveau Photography
Cover design by Larry Kuechlin

Gina Moreno

Contents:

07: Watermarks
10: Fragile
13: (BE)Longing
16: Transformation
18: Offering
20: Blue
23: Break
26: Ritual
28: Beat
30: Dissolve
32: Sacrifice
34: Storm
36: Reflections
38: Rain
40: The Depth of Water
42: Falling
44: Artfully Undone
46: Illuminate
48: Melt
50: Intensity
52: Cracked
54: Tides
56: Defined
58: Summer Sway
60: Dance (the Rain Soaked Night)
62: Whisper {Ombre Night}
64: Refuge (My Greatest Love)
66: 14 Lines
67: In Response

Gratitudes

Writing, a constant companion; though not always present, forever there. The words flow, through mind, soul and blood. Age 8, writing screenplays for my friends and myself to act out; 10 children's stories with my mom; as a teenager, poetry; an escape and vital release.

None of these have ever seen the light of day mind you. Until now, I never even believed it possible.

For several years, the ink dried up, but then my world came crashing down and I found myself wanting, needing to write. What you will find between these pages are pieces of me. I hope they bring a measure of beauty, comfort and perhaps a smile.

I am thrilled, humbled and honored to share a portion of the marks life has made on me.

Through the generosity, determination and gentle nudging of my dear friend Larry Kuechlin, this is all possible. Larry, thanks will never be enough. Your support, friendship, encouragement and never failing belief in me are a gift beyond measure. You pushed me to try harder, reach farther and never fear. My fellow oceansoul, thank you, always and ever.

Love and thanks to my family. You know what motivates me and my words; stand by me unconditionally and love me all the same.

Heartfelt gratitude and thanks as well to my friends and writers who inspire always

Nicole Chernick. Your words touch my soul and understand my heart. You know the pulse behind my words. We share, so much.

Jimmy Ray Davis. You always believed in me. Showed a scared and excited writer the way. An incredible mentor and friend.

Gina Moreno

Je' Maverick. My very first mentor. Your amazing words and friendship, a joy and means of providing me the necessary motivation to try. Your influence, priceless.

Caryl; my dear, sweet Princess. Always, always there for me. You too know the beat of my words. A gift you are.

Daniel; a constant support and undying friendship. I will probably never be able to thank you enough.

Ken; my dear friend. You know how much you mean to me. Constant. loyal, friend

R.G. Carroll; what can I say? Mentor, inspiration, dear friend. Your passion inspired me daily; your friendship, I will treasure forever

My fellow writers and soul sisters;

Patti, fellow sea sister, Jill, sister poet and wonderfully caring soul, Tawnya, we share more than many know. Diana Rose, strength and heart beyond measure. Leesah Santos, you show me how to be strong

The boys, Aaron, just wouldn't be as much fun without you. Dan Miles and Dan Kellet, your inspiration and talent never cease to amaze and inspire. Johnny, you were always there.

And to so many more who motivate me every day.

Gina Moreno
November, 2009

Watermarks

Gina Moreno

Watermarks

Listen closely;

the sound of sunset is an orchestra of hues
heart beats in time
playing notes that need no speech;
the touch will know its meaning.

Absorb the heat to taste the light dripping through the sky;

sunspill over skin is a rich honey flow
salt scent whisper;
circles around the head.

Moisture;

dew upon the skin; teardrops of the sun.
In this moment colors and scents
crash against available spaces
filling the void.

As the day melts across the sky,
taste the colors through the eyes.

Gold sinks below and light fades to water's edge;
sighing breeze as bare feet feel Earth's breathing.

Pressing ear to atmosphere, hear the rushing current;
heart needs the charge as waves to thirsty shore;

Watermarks

risk the drowning in their crashing.
Water on skin whispers silk to the senses;
slipping around flesh as silver drops fall from the sky.

Fingers of dusk

embroider gold and scarlet
through evenings velvet blanket;
pull edges over chilled skin.

End of day turns the sky inside out
and we become silhouettes in half light;
touched by the elements
and all that lies between.
No longer lost,
Sirius points the way
and in you I find home.

Sounds of sea echo words shared;
there is a pulse to the voice that turns
both ears and heart to its beat
underscoring the waves of its sound.

Grasp these notes that float between;
shape them into personal verse
drawn upon waiting skin;
water will wash over this parchment;
sky darkened by its stain.

Day now desires its new rhythm.

In your eyes reflected the dark moods of the sea;
for one moment I wish to drown in this madness
and perhaps be washed clean,

Gina Moreno

marked by your seal
staining the surface with your colors;

proof that what I know
is real.

This is our ocean

dive in and I will meet you somewhere in between.

Too long,
        separating intention and need

when all else fades to black

the only sound I hear becomes
the reason
        why I breathe.

Fragile

Living in a black and white world
tinged with traces of red
the colors of the soul,
through life have bled.

Walking around in a fog
lost in the night;
climb a high wire
through haze of pain
to blot out the fright.

Upended
broken from the inside
In this image of life
I am caught in the emulsion
while sand runs through the glass

My garden is watered by tears,
drops of me.

Pray for rain to quench the day
drench the flesh in streams of grey
wash away silverspun threads of lies;
at each broken promise
                    another piece dies.

Coiled

pressed between fingers of hurt and need
the addiction the emptiness did feed

Gina Moreno

An elixir for a waterless place
eyes black as coal puncture the skin
to feel strangely whole.

Unlaced

a splitting of seams
see visions in ink spots
swim in watercolor dreams.

The pulse

a drumbeat under skin
the addictions remain
only the form has changed.

The drug I now crave;

    the words
    the breath,

what little attention they gave.

Any words are better than being alone in my head.

If only to hide from the day
step away from the Sun;
to drown in the shadows,
escape from this game that I play.

My history is the dress I wear
the tales:
        ribbons braided through my hair.

Watermarks

Dressed up to put on the show
with each act denial will grow.

Need

to survive,
change.

Frozen skin waiting for the spark to set the fire within;
pressed lips to cold reality, where is warmth's taste.

Running in circles,
        how long can I hide from myself?

Tired of the fight
longing to find that pathway
 where my soul may be led
                      to cleanse;
lift the veil from my head.

Compassion comes kneeling.

Brave girl, I may trip, I may fall,
                      give in;
accept that I may not need
to be so tough after all.

If you wish to pick me up,
do not misread my stare;

for if you choose to do so
        please handle me with care.

Gina Moreno

[Be]longing

I had almost forgotten how to breathe...

    Your voice

Slowly, the rhythm returns

I.
What force causes the words
        hidden behind guarded lips to spill?
Cutting through phrase; freeing the blood
flow soul
flow meaning
      reaching in
to find how deep is the place from which it grows.

Grasp
envy the Sun its burn
pour
shine to light soul fire; tumbling gold to glass
sharpest angles compliment the curve
searching mirror for new reflection...
longing for a corner
in all the spaces in between.

II.
Breeze blows pushing pewter to obsidian hue.
Candles flicker light against the dark I call my night.

Watermarks

Sound
whiskey slide and flow;
as if fire beneath water;
with the quench
an underlying burn,
the touch
the music
of you.

Dreams traced on flesh;
the language of our souls
     ignite to burn
      indigo to ink.

Thumb press over breathing syllables,
smudging thoughts to blur
                              pull
the thread between spins tighter,
no longer certain where
          the seam of me ends

     and you begin.

Currents

when all that exists between lips and stare
    is a measure of static.

Will matched vibrations cause the senses to collide?

crash

connection

Gina Moreno

III.
Found.
Words.
Meaning.

      Listen closely,

you can hear the air sighing

      She belongs
           whispers the night

and in your gaze the words hold true.

I become
the parchment upon which to write.
Heat
    then bare shudder
upon my tongue
the weight of your name.

Hold.
Press.
Exhale;

melt
as the breath now takes the flame.

Transformation

If you drink in the light, will the colors change?
If you turn to the Sun, will the burn remain?

Drenched in tears, salt washes clean;
        naked, exposed, skin knows its calling
brittle are bones, worn by time.

Form.
Mold.
Recreate.

Tripping the line of chemistry's edge.
Somewhere between the line of gaze and catch of the blink,
impression made.

Found to envy the moon which, entranced,
licks the back, dripping over silvery curves
    eyes
            starlight on water.

Holding light in both hands;
if I gift you the Sun, will you color my night?
Crush topaz gold to paint opaque canvas;
stitch ebony with golden thread

Rough
chisel the edges; facet set to prism
resistance dissolves when the colors merge

Crush of mouth becomes

Gina Moreno

kiss of wine, running crimson round lips.
The drip of the berry is the potion divine.

Intake, but remember to exhale
as I collide with your air.
The meeting of lips is to touch not only the Sun
but to drown in its shade

When the tongue has lost its speech
teach the words once more.
Pause.
Breathe.

Transformed;
the way wax turns to melt when touched by the flame.
Day becomes night when swallowed by the Sun.
Stars burn when their course has run
 (the burn, the night, the wish).
A smudge on parchment that will not be ignored.
Crease on spine that cannot be unbent;
a cut, whose scar remains.

Cloak is now torn
shroud is rent;
push through.

Emerge
that I may reach the interior of the sky;
a flicker of wings,
though the butterfly makes no sound.

Show me heaven
that I may touch the ground.

Offering

She said she needed the journey.

Wind passes over trees, knowing;
echo of ghosts through weary bones.

After the burning; walking through what remains, the skin will meet the ashes. Spiraling back to tear, skinned, raw; the deepest layer of feeling.

Loosening ties that wind the wrists; palm scent, crush of gathered lilac. Slate is the color of the palette; dulled, scratch.

Armor. Permanent scar.

Cries pierce, slice, damage the air.

Searching for something sacred, something holy. Pull the rose that carries no scent for the one that bears the thorn. Precise is the pierce that sets the soul free; a wound that leaves no trace.

Heated is the vial that holds the spill, beware the burn of fingers pressed to curve where skin meets the lips. Elixir of vine and forbidden berry pushes ruby through lines that connect beat to the palms.

Uncurled, offering; broken bones will bleed.

That which drains from the soul, stains the atmosphere. Swallowing stars to feel their edge, gain warmth from the burn. Once written; sheets torn, pieces; tossing whisper to air.

Tightly woven fabric begins to unwind; there is comfort in the unbinding.

Stepping into the place where one confronts the other, stretches heartbeat to a line.

Gina Moreno

Set the flame, ignite the pulse. Give reason a name.

Face, a Titian painting;
         pale, resolute;
blushed in the knowing.
     Bare.

Laid to altar...

playing with the fire,
         blue sparks dance closest to the flame.
Burn   distort
   dissolve   recreate.

Syllables on parchment are
carved pieces of the heart
offered.
     Accept.
Touch and know their beat.

Wondering,   if only;

but

       will they?

Blue

Beneath the cerulean curtain;
deities painted in blue
speak of connection to

water   earth   life.

Brushing amethyst and gold;
tangled each
in others hold.
               Sunstruck,
scratch the surface
burn.

Naked souls
bare slide over rub of sand;
crushing shells
                 turn.

See the crashing waves
in sea green of eyes.
Kiss of salt to breaking surface;
                   yearn.

When circles deepen to indigo ink
what secrets
will they spill?

Loosen
bound fingers of hand;
    etch
promises to land.

Light caress to tilt of head
curve of back;
tracing the neck that is turning
to colors of Sun
burning.

Gina Moreno

Anointed, she drops,
cushioned by the sea;
liquid amber over crystal emerald rim;
tears the cloak,
setting soul free.

Sapphire is the
enamel painted
parchment
for which the touch has waited;

dreams curled in palms
that sing slow
and singe deep.

When smile captures fading light,
there is a burn
          in between

just at the edge of the fingertips
heat sparks the air,
causing edges to curve

a song flowing ,
riding over tongue
drenching the surface;
crystal cut.

Pour words of starlight
drunk on vocabulary, flow
over the rim,
staining the edges;

kiss
cobalt fire from lips
                  red;
rush of blue;

moon flirting with clouds
washes skin in silver light;
streak the surface,

Watermarks

a blur of starlight

etch the story,
tear the surface;
        complicate the plot.

Night exhales its fragrance;
disturbance
melt into darkness;
this is the pool
in which we swim.

The rush of water
is the wash of moonlight;

cleanse
swallow;

a blend of breath and whisper,   air
to reach the deepest places

submerge   succumb   release

dipped in indigo
        immortal

breathe
and float
to the surface.

Gina Moreno

Break

I stare through the grey that slivers the azure sky...

Lips pressed to window wish only to breathe
pure
once
more

Eyes stained by ink that pours from the soul long to see
clear
once
more

Curve of ears crave to hear
sound
once
more

The edges are smudged to grey; a charcoal reminder of where
the fire once burned

You wish to bind me, ankles and wrists
with words
                words...
words that promise warmth, but leave only shadow

Over the edge;
push and empty the well of its ink
        clinging to the fingers,
seeps
permanent stain
remains.

Smeared pain to curled parchment,
I write
and write...

Watermarks

This is the thumb press to the heart;
the lines that come from the core;
the ebony flow.

When did the thirst for raven turn to gold?

A desire for ruby
the taste of wine
becomes uncertain;
a crossing of the line.

Slip of lips;
bite of tongue,
a thirst for red
left standing to swallow
all that could not be said.

Searching for the burn
through the thinnest red line.
Grasping the dagger;
which way will it turn?

Pointed;
the verse leaves its mark.
Fierce;
I have cut my teeth on sharper souls.

Exposed;
slice the straps, drop the cloak
reach up
slit the clouds to beg for the bleed of water
that washes sin clean.

Sliding through air
to burn with the sun;
my heart beats
but the blood knows not where to run.

I will not be stretched to fit
the canvas of your dream.
Live with this stain;

Gina Moreno

let the colors run,
absorb into skin.

Cut;
let the quill pierce the vein;
pulse
there is poetry in this body.

Broken promises laid to altar
strike the match and burn every line.
Unwrap this melancholy gift.

Refine;

unloose the ties that bind
the flesh to bone;
the beat to forbidden rhyme

Break;
walk away;
your call to the wind will not cause my turn

not
     this
          time...

Ritual

In the dark the soul seeks asylum
in the light, it faces need.

Awaken to a beat, too loud to ignore
when the skin calls for the weight of the hand.
Hunger laid at altar; drink deep the elixir
let the cleansing begin.

Shroud of fear presses passion within.
When given the chance,
would you change the shape of water
or risk the crash of fall?

Cast all   Sacrifice   Chill

Longing for heat;
       we swallow the sun

Lit;
scarlet burns to blue, tinged with gold;
fire to soul
spark the charcoal remains.
Tracing lines in the ash;
burnt fingers
the reminder...scar

Melt

Pour
the rush;
grasp with both palms
all that lies in between

Push
the edge
that slides through the blades;
the cut true, clean

Gina Moreno

Bleed

Air breaks to glass;
    slice
impression is made

This is the place where the line breaks
translate each syllable to yearning, need
draw blood from once empty page
Mouth forms shape over words;
bite and feel the bleed

Twist
now the snake
will handle its charmer.
Color skin
with pomegranate seed;
touch and the stain remains.

Pulling ink from the sky;
parched lips drink moon water
Burn hands on fire of star;
it is only these tips that can sharpen the edge.

With this point, one makes their mark.

What remains; it was never a lie;

    the angel with broken wings
    has earned the right to cry.

Shadow dance;
kiss the places where morning deepens.
Finding rhyme in the wash of water;

Bend   Turn   Kneel

Breathe....Let go
                        Liquefy

Beat

Listen for the sound
just below silence,
it is the breath of the heart
beating to draw vital air;

the hum of the song that passes between
when black falls and stars paint silver to ebony stare.

To touch is to feel the sky

when dream is
what slips beneath the curve of the eye.

Pulling on bands of silk
        how softly ribbons fall.

Skin
polished ivory under quiver of palm;
fingers respond
        to longing hearts call.

Rhythm of beat,
sweep, the fall of hair
            exhale
bringing sound to once silent air

Thirst;
long for the pull of richest wine;
crystal kiss to ruby stain;
drinking the breath that dwells beneath the line.

Gina Moreno

How can heat run
in the chill of exposure?
Whispering words into skin,
running current to the core.

Blue crack of lit match
piercing honeypoured eyes.

Fingerslide;
quick scratch, barely a mark
but ever a shudder;

fire to the flesh
trace the line
that runs between the blades.

Subject of desire;
study of art;
soul pierced by a passionate wire.

While candle melts slowly
focus on the center of light.
Painting with touch only one can master

Strokes of brush
give passion a name,
forever painted on shape of this frame

This art,
canvas burnt edges in a moment of fire

The colours
this flesh will now wear,
and even after the stars
the beat is still there.

Dissolve

Cinema
behind the dark of eyelids,
visions crisscross

red, orange, blazes of yellow;
pierce the tiny lines
from which the blood flows...

Fiber by fiber, reason snaps
a strand pulled too tightly

Darkness eats at the edge of reason;
draws black over bluest of eyes

Breathe deeply the innocent breeze;
it knows not the sins of the heart
Dark is the shape of the dreams

The rush
from the head to the core;
is the blackest of streams

Unbound
flesh uncurls exposed

Bare parchment waiting, anticipating

Tip the fountain
pour the blood;
a spreading ink stain

Push then pull quill
for fear the point
will scratch through the paper

Chilled
stretch the dark pathway;
pulling ghosts from inside

Gina Moreno

Surrounded by mirrors;
reflection in dark spaces
light is

the shine of the moon
swimming under glass
Find substance in shadows

Drink deep
finding richness within;
There is more to this marrow

Caught in the web
of truth and distinction;
soul needs the elements in between

Naked feet
search the press of cold;
sense in the chill

Knowing full well
the kiss of frost,
can be lethal to the vine

The cut of cold
rushes force to the heart,
awakens the soul

Shock to the system;
without the beat,
there can be no pulse at all

Search for the place where
the ice cracks
slip in and dissolve

Risking the crash that comes with the fall
This liquid connection better than
                              no hold at all.

Sacrifice

Search,
broken and burnt;
down the deep pathway
naked feet over stone...

Under canopy of coppershot lavender,
laced with blood crimson;
strike match that will singe orange to thick air.

In the melt of wax there is recognition;
burn reminds the soul it is still alive.

As the colors change,
I find you somewhere between
the blue and the red
Melt the veil that lies across skin
Cut the sky open to shower with dust of stars;
tracing constellations on this fleshly plane

Step into indigo
before comes the dark

As breeze brushes across
feel slow step along spine
Destiny trails her finger
Become
flames
a white fire along veins
Strip the layers to lay naked heart;
bending at the foot of this Earthly altar

Gina Moreno

Kiss of night to parched lips pulls
what can no longer be contained.

Twirl and taste
the shape of name upon tongue;
drink of the richest wine.

Blood pushes beat
An offering of palms;
    desire
    divine
Release jagged pieces in hands;
the comfort in pain
accept what I am;
wash the stain clean

Curling into pocket of night
soul becomes fluid;
dressed in melt of mist,
liquid runs over curve:

the arch is the bridge to the dream.

Awaken to caramel glow;
drink deep the drops of dawn
as Sun rubs dark from the sky;
a hint of flush crosses the scars that I wear

the ghosts now defeated.

Touch,
but do not form me fragile
even glass bends when heated.

Watermarks

Storm

Chilled:

the press of clouds deliver the storm
on the edge of evening;
a disturbance of color;
spider weave of webs through dream
silken chords pull the edges.

Echoes:

the snap before electrical frame.
When the wind meets resistance
you can hear the breeze whisper.

Pressing palms to air, lest the sky should fall.

Throwing arms around emptiness,
fingercurl grasp of that which slides between.

Reach to scrape the ebony, leaving silver marks;
there is comfort in the scratch.

Memories are scars;
when fingers run over
tracing marks that tell story.
The coiled soul will bite in due time.
Clocks speak the mystery
as they bend with each rhyme.

Remains:

the scrape of red over shoulder and breast;
the place where arrow made its mark
just short of the piercing.

Write

red upon the blue lines;
this fold in soul
will time unbend?
Slice open the words
yet beware
you do not slip on the pour.
The slide of water is
silver string symphony through velvety black;
curve of ears pull the sound
as the slow crawl of rain
inches over this surface.
Drifting on the painted horizon
gold and green,
the contour of water
meets curl of the flame.
Watching in slow motion
as glass pours the sand;
stretch for the half open door;
reality breaks surface
of this watercolor dream:

pull pen
push paper
breeze washes in...

scattered pages on the floor.

Reflections

I etch a name in the clouded mirrors
in the fogveiled windows
on the icy surface upon which I stand.

I hear the sound of you in
the pressing of trees against the wind;
blue deep is the color of the day in which we drown.
Open eyes to cold hour;
pulling apart the layers of complicated dreams;
nocturnal secrets will pour from this vial of time.

Is it possible to breathe in a glance so deeply
that its meaning absorbs the being?
Pray each look is not the beginning of the lie.
Hushed breath, slow spill;
how smoothly the words roll over the tongue.
Air weeps the music as the soul stirs the sound;
which notes will be hung upon the sky?

Will a moon swollen with tears
shed the water beg from the face of the heavens
to wash the sin which on burning skin lies?
The heart beats the truth; essence beneath
flesh cries.

Scratch the surface to see the words the veins will spell;
laced with fire
singe the lines in between.

Gina Moreno

Burnt paper curls at the edges, yet the heat remains;
beware the embers--
tiny sparks long for flames

When does self overpower need;
the slice become necessary;
does it quench the thirst to watch the bleed?

Naked soul stroll through sacred garden;
grasp the rose, scratch the thorn;
bitter is the bite, but sweet is the flower.
Caress the petal, leaving thumbprints in the dew.
Cast stones upon glass lake;
beg for a vision that is new.

Stand before glass, lift the veil from heavy eyes.
See not only the outlines, but the colors in between.

Too long chasing the light to find where the shadow falls;
the weight is bent branch on the verge of breaking.
Beg the stars to receive what the Earth cannot hold;
night turns hollow where there is no sound;
colors are shaken
and the name is changed.

Broken,
we become
mosaic
in dust and painted fragments lie
but in the remains I see,
reflections
jeweled pieces
of me.

Rain

There is a flow that runs over skin and quenches the soul...

Deepest blue;
              interrupted ,
cut by flinty grays.

Clouds crash to release their fill;
 sky colors pewter
as the silver drops fall.

Rushing air is the breath of the wind
Clouds touch down, teasing treetops;

shivering breeze;
              nature sighing

Violet shadows dance against the sharp, hard edges
Impression etched upon cold air

Contact
      lightning strike ;
    touch
              stare

eyes turn to color of the sea in winter;

crash of the storm; rush of water
slide over skin to pool at dancing feet
arch and twirl.

Gina Moreno

Liquid folds; a wave of wash to mouth
Caught up in the current;
the weight is that of water upon thirsty skin

     contact
heat
         turn to vapor

Stretching fingertips to atmosphere
write words on page of sky
lines run an azure script.

Thunderstruck,
     breath taken
  exhale
         and send it back to me

count the trembling stars;
         a glistening crescendo
sink in clouds of charcoal silver;

can you hear the moon exhale?

Listen to natures call
pressed flesh to Earth
leaves impression on wet grass

     remain

dressed in scent and sheen;
veiled in

the afterfall.

Watermarks

The Depth of Water

The Sun will kiss the clouds, smiling for the weight of it.

As rose drops dew,
air sighs, setting color to the atmosphere.
Water drives,
alone knowing the way it turns

    Immerse
inhale
        dive in.

Push pulse to flow; drums the crimson core
runs currents through the blood
to meet at the point where the beat begins.
Strike harmony in silent chords,
there is music in the breeze.

Pressed by shadows, sway to find
comfort in the curve of the heart;
tapping into the center, where need can barely contain;
a spill to quench thirst,
a pulse to sustain.

The blaze of falling stars will singe the skin
while lighting fire to the eyes.
Weigh the choices;
jewels will cause the sparkle
yet the flint will cause the flame.

Gina Moreno

A dance of winds that play
from heat the air will tremble.
Wave washes over; wrapped round in azure arms
salt press to breathing shore;
the pull of moons late burning.

Lip place words upon the throat
grasp meaning before they take shape;
flowing stream to waiting heart.

Night slips
loose gown from shoulders fall;
the silk that drops,
a whisper to naked feet;
waiting air, exhales.

Float,
while trying to touch bottom.

The breath, the lines, the waves
ebb and flow
wind over treetops continues to blow;
Nature's truth
the soul longs to know.

The importance of gravity;
the moment you discover where the sunlight falls;
the pull of the ocean when the wind calls;
the need to fly while in you I drown.

It is
the weight of the wind
and the depth of water.

Falling

Can you taste it in the air?
Cinnamon and spice;
        summer heat tinged by crisp chill...

Follow the path of tangled streets;
lamp lit and music led; in the air there is a turning.
Summer sheen becomes skin waiting for the warming
and the tunes take new meaning.

        Glow in golden light;

pull pieces of setting sun
to draw on skin a rich orange hue.
These fingers of light are the angels caress;
weaving wings with golden thread;
an embrace that lingers on shoulders curve
and causes dip in the breath;
set fire to this parchment;
beating heart will take the flight.

Breeze shakes the trees;
russets, coffee and citrine; tiny flags in changing light:
they are the whispers of each kiss;
they are promises of time

Spun gold and jewels; a honeyed illumination,
fall colors to summer satin drip from the skin
leaving shadows in their wake in these dreams lie,
feeding on the colors cast.

Gina Moreno

Day turns topaz silk to azure velvet cloak,
studded with silver dreams of new beginnings;
hope, woven deep with the colors;
in the fabric of the smile, lips form a crimson curve.

Scent of sensation drips rich in thick air
saturated by the wine and whiskey hues;
drunk on the colors, the taste that courses through the veins
becomes a feast for the heart.

Partake;

column of neck leads to curve below
single touch tracing back ignites blood lines to fire;
as I step into the flame, feel the heat from my burn.

The moment when you forget how to breathe

the weight of it bends time in half;
beg it stand still that we may shatter into the crisp new air,
becoming one with the atmosphere;
a gift to the season.

As the sun winks at the silvery sky
and the leaves sing their turning;
wrap lips around the taste;
find warmth in the burning;

open smoky eyes
to realize
this is
the

falling.

Artfully Undone

    Perception   imagination   sketch

write
        weave
  paint
        me...

The words; colors of the palette;
subtle slice of knife,
the visible scars show how deeply I am touched.
Drawn upon the skin,
     fleshmarks;
the chalk lines, a caress to paper;
scratch, and the mark is made.

Trace the delicacy of figures to mirror the intent;
     unhinged;
will you slip me from my frame?
Chip away the paint
        to find the texture underneath?

Though I can never fit in your corners,
grant me the spaces in between
Breath to fill the atmosphere;
moves across the heart, giving rhythm to its beat
Soul song sung as you walk across this valley,
tread softly on its curve

Create
grind the colors in the bowl

Gina Moreno

Write
trace notes upon the flesh
A tapestry of fire,
pull the golden thread
Watch
colors of souls will run

Hand to skin
Paint to canvas
Lit match to waiting wick
In the glow of this warmth swept away by the blaze;
become the burn to my landscape.

Fingers pressed to the parchment;
colors running over edge;
smudge the lines
Muse will bite the ankles
and bring us to our knees

Rapid beating heart strains fabric of the dress,
hand stills at jaw;
over lip caress paint sensation, layer by layer;
ruby ring on waiting finger.
There is a rushing;
flow colors over white tide

Resistance lies on cold floor;
white chalk line pressed in folds of linen,
silver sheen to umber spine.

Visualized   realized   immortalized

    moonstunned;
        artfully
              undone.

Illuminate

I carry an angel of fire and an angel of ice;
to which do I succumb?

As a result of sins the blood runs cold
and a taste of ash lies upon the tongue.
In the reaching for heaven, I have bent the stars;
the weight of my wishes, unable to contain.
A Temple built within, I bring flowers of promise to its altar;
kneeling in nocturnal corners;
praying for that which washes clean.

Trapped behind my own reflection,
there is a line drawn before the glass;
when crossed will it be shattered;
setting the demons free?

I am drawn upon the aubergine sky;
chasing the electrical currents that slice through the rich velvet
dreams; internal storm collision,
a temporary flash of light.
Around sharp corners,
a release from dark night
the one who has palms of light;
the sound of a voice that rushes over; water to quench the thirst,
careful to breathe between each sip;
lost in strong embrace; hands to skin
a communion of trust.

At this dark temple, fragile lies beneath the eyes;
pull the ghosts from deep inside.

Gina Moreno

Dressed in dark despair; slip ribbons from this fabric,
place upon skin's parchment, a promise.

Words, worn as pendant around neck, warming that which it
caresses; setting fire within.

A small breath of hesitation, inhale every line
for words soothe the pain;
risk the pull that may break the chain.

Pressed against stone wall draped heavy in vines;
words, choicest grapes upon claret lips
      the shadow of a kiss;
    aftertaste
           light fire to the eyes

You,
the moon that bleaches the darkness,
paints silver to my black sky:
lift the dark curtains;
mark the pathway to the light.
Could this be redemption;
measure reinvented, reason defined?

Draw out the colors you know exist;
pull light from deepest well.
My soul this chance may save; cut deep
tap the vein that bleeds the truth;
once lost now unafraid
stretch out the hand
as fragile love
steps away

from the grave.

Melt

It is deep summer, drowning in the tangerine and gold;
blues buzz background;
                weeping guitar hum.

Follow the straight path down the sultry crooked alley;
        stretch to touch the other side.
Led by the sounds, lost in the tune.

Pull clouds for the moisture; moon tilts to heady air.
In this atmosphere everything changes,
                sounds intensify, colors deepen.
There is a message in the sky; will you reach out to trace it?
It draws the path from me to you.

Fingers translate a wordless hunger; rich language in thick air
searching for translation; rouge lips
                the words will know

Spills the inky hue, quill scratch to fresh skin;
will it breathe soul to the paper?

Am I lost if taken in?

Lightning flash, there is a thunder within;
shaken by the turning; spark match to still air.
Ignite; turn sight to candlelight;
there is a pulse to curling flame
the heart beats syllables of your name.

Gina Moreno

Have you heard the sound of blood, its rush to destination;
there is a signal through the fire;
                          for you I'd risk the burn.

Travel through the white night that we may color the edges;
a ruby scratch on open surface; though the mark fades,

       sensation remains.

Along the lines, play the melody of summer rain;
1000 tiny drops become the souls tapping refrain.
Trace lines from the center to the bottom,
an imaginary fishnet seam.

Palm to palm; the lines, a map to the heart;
skin to skin, touch; the journey to the soul.
Scan horizon of the flesh to find the setting sun;
an intensity to shatter shadows.

As scent of tomorrow hangs lush in the air,
graze the candles flicker, swallow the heat

feel the glow,
absorb the hue

for at the touch of the flame

we will melt into
                the blue.

Intensity

Lost in the deep, we long to take flight...

There is a touch that fills the spaces,
                words that tease the soul.
The heart is a hungry animal,
it will consume to feel whole.
It is to heat as red is to fire;
                recognize the colors.

The body is a parchment on which to draw the lines;
can one find the map to the centre?

Chilled hands slide; attempt to start the flame.

Shake the vial that stands unbroken,
unsettle the atmosphere.
Internal storm; examine the landscape
drops of lightning, set fire to the plane.

There is a tune to the pulse of blood;
press ear to wrist; can you feel the beat?
A deep echo that touches the bottom of the soul.

Body language speaks words
the mouth has not yet spoken;
                      read the signs.

Run fingertips to rose, slide and risk the thorn
Beware, the knife slice of passion cuts both ways.

Gina Moreno

A rise and dip on angels wings;
touch and pull stars from the hair,
                      caught in the floating.
A ghost of you moves through me:
        what do you see on the other side?

An afterimage on the silent screen
which memory will not erase;
feel the heat as we swim through the static.

A need for air, the knowledge of being;
inhale and reach to grasp the fluid things:

sliding into the velvet
                      moondrowned

Intensity:
a crashing of two in need.

White stars burn above the wreck
heart strings pull night from beginning to end

and so we rise, soulsong to sing
heat kisses cold edges;
and with warm breeze
flutters the wing.

Watermarks

Cracked

On the windows that are the eyes, there is a crack along the pane

Tears that dress the lashes become the drops that fall to bare shoulders;
the absent touch
I am aware
In the pressure, the our glass has cracked.

You;
    running sand through fingers; the hold is lost
    Tear candles wick to kill the flame, when light is clouded,
    no sense of shadows remain

Marks have been made with fine edged words
made sharp on stone of heart.

A suffocation of terms, they slide from the ears to hold the throat
    The map drawn on my back would not lead to my heart
    the truth you did not know:
    why pierce the skin to grasp the flow?
Lost within the syllables, searching for
the what, when, where and how
                    of why.

Caught between the lines;
torn paper, folded pieces.
Heart in hand, crushed by the curling;
    don't ask me to shoulder your heaven,
    I'm still trying to scratch the stars.

Gina Moreno

The painted wings now broken.
I never claimed to be that angel,

but rather
a leaf separated from the tree,
struggling in the floating;
trace the veins to feel the lines of me.

Echoes,
    broken soul frequency;
    surrounding space crumbles
the leftover bits, a mosaic will now make.

Puzzle piece
        vision;
cracked
        mirror reflects;
broken glass,
beware the   cut
when trying
to
      pick
  up
     the
    pieces

Watermarks

Tides

We will meet in a place called Summer

Many are the wishes cast to unfolding waves.
Hope: you can hear it in the sound of the sea,
you have only to listen
                with desire.
We stand at the center, as broken shells along the shore;
finding beauty in the pieces.

Sun weaves citrus through russet sky,
thread warmth to flowing sea
Tides turn to sloping green,
pour brilliant gold to glisten the blue.
There is a soft silence;
can you hear the sounds that pass between two breaths?
A seaspun exhalation.
If you listen carefully to the naked voice,
you can hear the shape of the heart

Pull essence from the air to spice the skin,
savor the salty scent
The fire will burn the way the hands have taught it.
With the glow; day slips slowly to horizon and resistance
loses shape

Skin to shimmer from clinging mist,
there is a spinning of wonder;
dew trapped in spiders web
slip waterfalls of lace as
seaspray glisten to face.

Gina Moreno

You are the silvershine glimpse
through my darkest clouds;
drops of light to atmosphere.

We waterdance below curious sky;
look closely; the stars are smiling.

Woven of time and promises,
we become our own tapestry;
captured by the gesture of the hand,
the curve of the smile
and the glint of the eye,
pull tight the final string.

Desire exists behind the eyes of reason,
look and you will see it there.

      We will find it
somewhere between
the rich earth and cobalt sky;
where there is a rushing of tides
that push and pull
without asking why.

Defined

Help me understand
the beat of the heart,
the touch of the hand.

By light of parchment shade,
curled candles flame;
absorb the heat; hold it:
a fire that defines the night
stone to stone touch,
                        spark;
golden-edged ebony and light
downward candle burn,
sink soft to amber glow.

Hold back the arms of clock,
for time is flexible and I will bend with you.

Hearts unfold as beats shift in the dark.
Touch will fill the fragile frame,
a healing balm for the burnt places.

The canvas is hand colored,
paint beyond the lines
blend light to tawny skin;
colors; senses entwine.
Scrape of nail to shoulder bare,
        quill scratch;
lines drawn.

Gina Moreno

A song
not to sing, but to define emotion;
the notes will overflow,
soft; liquid slow:
a voice which leaves footprints
upon the soul.

Trace heart;
finger touch to skin,
it's rhythm, a statement beyond language;
once incomplete, now touched entirely.

    Wish;

for just one moment to be your air,
the need which sustains you

Awaiting the other side of night;
press words to rest softly upon curve of the ear.

On your voice spirit will dine;
with the eyes,
    form outlined;

and in your smile

I am
    defined.

Summer Sway

The pulsing rhythm slices through the muggy air:

beskirted legs
        twist and twirl; flash bare honey skin.
Abandon starched linen and lace,
pull ribbons from the hair;
an ebony cascade.

Her laughter draws magic from the air;
she is the silver tongued angel,
        adorned with broken wings:
the vibrant glow, lighting his dark night.

She wears a dress of simple blue:
                lightning strike
emerald eyes flash fire in the watching:
mesmerized by the stars in her eyes.

Ignoring the glances of many, she turns
to the lonely boy in the corner
finger extend, point and curl:

    Come dance with me...

Drop match to the fire,
        turn up the flame
palms bend to curve of flesh,
summer heat
slow drop and slide down spine,
glistening release.

Gina Moreno

She moves fluid, brandy smooth;
                a 3 finger to bare wrist pour:

   jasmine scent, heady
   essence of the moment,
   taste the cinnamon air.

Trace the thin blue line leading straight to the heart
strum the brown-eyed blues
coffee dark eyes
              see only him.

Caught in the rhythm and music,
bodies form a single note, beating
so plays the fevered heart
as lone guitar weeps,
             they fashion metaphors
crystal to lips,   slip the whiskey slide;

a new path has been laid
they would not trade a moment
for this kiss along the blade.

It is on this edge they find the map to the center
as each soul in turn refines the other.

Whisper to ear:

Why me; the lonely boy in the corner,
who most choose not to see?

From curving cherry lips the reply:

     It was your silence: in volumes it spoke to me.

Dance (the rain-soaked, jazz night)

We could have listened all night, drown in the pulse and the
rhythm that sets the soul afire.

It was a night when the rain washed the sky;
                        falling , slanting waterfalls, veils of grey
silk thread from spun clouds adorning velvet curtain above.

The moon a luminous smile against this ebony sky;
                                     confident in its knowing.

We walked,
      then ran down dark alley, aware of the soaking, yet
uncaring, through silver reflecting pools at feet, seeking the
sanctuary of four walls.
                    Walls that would smile upon our joy;
      absorb the laughter, observe the dance.

Glistening wet runs down dark hair, sliding over shoulders, a
temporary sheen. Remove the sheath to reveal, the warmth
underneath. Grab the night and wrap selves within it.

Through cracked window pane,
drift sounds of the city, the night, rich warm
                                       Coltrane .

Softly mingled against shadows, in the heart the words are
underlined. Hands ache in the need to trace, to touch, to feel.
The fevered heart beats its own song, longing,
                          share this dance with me.

Gina Moreno

Swing in slow, lazy sway, place hands to ivory key. Imagine the spine, a curved saxophone, touch of fingers upon it speaking louder than sound,

flowing through the veins to flood the heart with
                                                            song.

On this sheet music, we play our part. Upon the once dark night, rich colors now flow, the skin a canvas, here a new tune begin, scratch notes in the corners,
                as the body becomes the art.

We could have danced all night...

Dawn breaks, sun kisses moon goodnight. Dragging the evening sky with it, the light passes by pillowed heads, spreading over them, gossamer threads to capture starkissed dreams.

Exhale of breath, a shared sigh.

Two souls, twin notes now read and the cool blue jazz echoes softly, sweetly, still dancing in our heads.

Whisper {Ombre Night}

Bronze shadows slide over whitewashed walls
smear gold to glisten skin
Stain of setting sun turns to dusting of moonlight
lost in the sultry, delicious
                         ombre' night
Moon sends the wish as fingers of palm hinge
to catch the falling star

 Taste evening of rich red wine,
red blanket, enfold in scarlet hue
Slow sliding smile, flex of mouth
sparks ignite the eyes
Blackberries adorn fruited lips
to kiss the honeyed tune
Hearts and breath a medleyed sound

I become the song you wish to sing
a slow blues hum, slide and strum
drown deep within your air

A barefoot twirl on sinking floors,
gravity unknown

    to touch
    to hands
    to heart
    to soul

Gina Moreno

The flooding heart wishes to speak,
                               wait
pressed gently fingers across mouth
say not a word,
                listen
the sound of human voice,
a necessary obsession.
      Trace trembling throat
escaping tears,
liquid drops of joy unknown
kiss the salty rims
                 slip the silk
press quill to seams
     tilt the halo,
script exquisite scenes

Each whisper touch to waiting ear
uttered word by word
                     deep within, a fire,
the breath, the phrases stirred
stand fixed in light of candle
palm shadows with both hands
                            inhale
through lips passes my name
                     exhale
      extinguish trembling flame.

Once soul-sealed,
now within the lock has turned the key
and time will not erase this memory,
                         this moment

the night he whispered

me.

Watermarks

Refuge (My Greatest Love)

A beckoning, a yearning;
souls refuge the purest passion.

    Escape;

when no one else is listening, I turn to thee...

In colors I drown,
entwine me in seaweed grasp
heat the surface with sandpaper scratch;
ginger-hued parchment sky
clouds slash with brushstrokes
of cranberry stain and violet dye
cerulean blue, passionate artist hue
a beauty so piercing like a lightning strike,
slicing one in two, intensity,
                    fireflame blue.

Here the starving soul is warmed and fed
where even the air is grateful for the chance to breathe
windswept, salt-tipped mist.
The sand, a canvas upon which to mark my sins.
To the waves I whisper my song;
the swell is all too aware for what I long.
Upon the wet sand I lie,
lost in thought as ocean comes and goes
drenches the hair and licks the toes.

Finger breezes dip and lift sprays
to christen skin with crystal droplets touch.

Gina Moreno

The waves crest, a surge of hope for the heart.
Clouds fold, a golden light
to set down upon obsidian pool below.

    Sun kisses sea.
A shiver, not a chill
but fascination as sunset bleeds into water
casting shimmering hues,
            a jewelbox night
pearl orb suspended in a velvet sky
pierced by singing stars;
my ears absorb their chorus.
Here is a darkness I wish not to escape
Envelope self in its satin touch evening,
a phantom kiss, seaspun rush.

How can one not be inspired?
For in the sun and moon, stars and watery deep

    poetry is alive:
        it etches itself into me;
        were you to cut me open,
        I believe
            I would bleed the sea.

As another day comes to an end;
broken heart, a stitch closer to mend.
A saltlick brush upon damp lips
warm wind breath upon the skin.

Here I feel, here I mend and always
  the sea   my soul
      needs to

            breathe in.

14 Lines

Night inks spiders web, gossamer thread to capture soul
prick the night with pulse of light; spin and sink to crystal deep.
Learn the rhythm of breathing, choose future hour to sleep;
become temptation best not accept at once impossible to forget.

Moth to flame, risk fire to feel the burn;
movements beneath surface feed blood to vital heart,
                                      push the rushing flow.
Lift beyond the ordinary things;
teach what more there is to know;
chords of deep music scratch the silence:
heart sings; beg pull the strings.

Distillation; drink deep essential elements;
trace lips, define the russet curves; here smile is drawn.
Smooth lines of neck; breathe, soft turn to the dawn.
Broken rays spark the burning;
life script between pages, found in turning.

Cracked mirror understands meaning within the eyes;
look closely, heart beats between the lines

Gina Moreno

In Response

In response

to the one who stole the rose's red
leaving merely thorns to cut
bleeding out the innocence within
wilted, ground rose to dust
tears freely fell
footprints left on muddy edge of soul
hard press thumb to clay heart
impression, lasting
shattered.

What remains
a residue of dreams upon broken glass soul
from cuts, life's joy did flow.

Bathe in tears of the forsaken,
washing the red to blue
undue pain, caused by you,
forgotten

The past reflects endlessly in corners of faded mirrors,
no longer can I face their stare.

Can you hear the faint voice?

It is the heart calling,
rushing though the blood, reaching through the soul
pleading, dying to be heard.

Watermarks

Enough

Too long lonely dancing in the dark,
the heart needs the Sun
for what is love without the
complimentary shadows

    Then came you.

In response
        to your warmth
the shuddering daybreak
 when the heat of sun touches chill of night

Uncurl the folded hands
        too long gripping the unknown
strong fingers relieve the weariness,
lace together to lead home

A smile that defines the moon,
                eyes that rival the stars
within your atmosphere,
exposed I roam

the need to trust,   yet still uncertain:

in response...

    I beg

please do not set me up to fall
with words too kind,
        caressing
which I may not live up to
    or fit into their skin

Gina Moreno

rather
      accept me for what I can only be

a humble vessel for your liquid beauty
the words that flow from silver tongue,
they are the balm that soothes me.

No longer shedding tears
for the one forgotten
          or who I used to be;

I become the word which passes through your lips,

          friend

it's meaning I now truly learn
and in response

to you

      I turn.

Watermarks

Gina Moreno

www.ingramcontent.com/pod-product-compliance
Lightning Source LLC
Chambersburg PA
CBHW060426050426
42449CB00009B/2151